Audition Songs for Male & Female Singers
Gilbert & Sullivan

Ten classic songs
ideal for auditions

Wise Publications
London/New York/Paris/Sydney/Copenhagen/Madrid/Tokyo

Exclusive Distributors:
Music Sales Limited
8/9 Frith Street,
London W1D 3JB, England.
Music Sales Pty Limited
120 Rothschild Avenue,
Rosebery, NSW 2018,
Australia.
Music Sales Corporation
257 Park Avenue South,
New York, NY 10010, United States of America.

Order No. AM958188
ISBN 0-7119-8215-5

Music processed by Enigma Music Production Services
CD backing tracks arranged by John Maul.
Front cover photograph (The Pirates Of Penzance) courtesy of Rex Features.
Back cover photographs courtesy of Arena Images.
With thanks to Chris Butler for suggesting the addition of this title to the series.

Printed in the United Kingdom by
Caligraving Limited, Thetford, Norfolk.

I Am The Very Model Of A Modern Major-General

Words by W.S. Gilbert
Music by Sir Arthur Sullivan

in - for - ma - tion ve - ge - ta - ble, an - i - mal, and mi - ne - ral: I
an - swer hard a - cros - tics; I've a pret - ty taste for pa - ra - dox; I
know the kings of Eng - land, and I quote the fights his - to - ri - cal, From
quote, in e - le - gi - acs, all the crimes of He - lio - gab - a - lus; In
Ma - ra - thon to Wa - ter - loo, in or - der ca - te - go - ri - cal; I'm
con - ics I can floor pe - cu - li - ar - i - ties pa - ra - bo - lous; I can
ve - ry well ac - quaint - ed, too, with mat - ters math - e - ma - ti - cal, I
tell un - doubt - ed Ra - pha - els from Ger - ard Dows and Zof - fa - nies I

un - der - stand e - qua - tions, both the sim - ple and quad - ra - ti - cal, A -
know the croak - ing cho - rus from the Frogs of Ar - is - toph - a - nes! Then
a tempo
- bout bi - no - mial the - o - rem I'm teem - ing with a lot o' news, With
I can hum a fugue of which I've heard the mu - sic's din a - fore, And
ma - ny cheer - ful facts a - bout the square of the hy - po - te - nuse.
whis - tle all the airs from that in - fer - nal non - sense, Pin - a - fore!
Chorus
With ma - ny cheer - ful facts a - bout the square of the hy - po - te - nuse, With
And whis - tle all the airs from that in - fer - nal non - sense, Pin - a - fore, And
f

ma - ny cheer - ful facts a - bout the square of the hy - po - te - nuse, With
whis - tle all the airs from that in - fer - nal non - sense, *Pin - a - fore,* And
ma - ny cheer - ful facts a - bout the square of the hy - po - te - po - te - nuse.
whis - tle all the airs from that in - fer - nal non - sense, *Pin - a - pin - a - fore.*
fz
I'm ve - ry good at in - te - gral and dif - fe - ren - tial cal - cu - lus; I
Then I can write a wash - ing bill in Ba - by - lon - ic cu - nei - form, And
pp
know the sci - en - tif - ic names of be - ings a - ni - mal - cu - lous:
tell you ev - 'ry de - tail of Ca - rac - ta - cus - 's u - ni - form:
In

short, in mat - ters ve - ge - ta - ble, an - i - mal, and mi - ne - ral, I
am the ve - ry mo - del of a mo - dern Ma - jor - Gen - er - al.
Chorus
f
In
short, in mat - ters ve - ge - ta - ble, an - i - mal, and mi - ne - ral, He
f
is the ve - ry mo - del of a mo - dern Ma - jor - Gen - er - al.

Slower
3. In fact, when I know what is meant by
pp
"ma - me - lon" and "ra - ve - lin", When I can tell at sight a Mau - ser
ri - fle from a ja - ve - lin, When such af - fairs as sor - ties and sur -
- pris - es I'm more wa - ry at, And when I know pre - cise - ly what is

meant by "com - mis - sa - ri - at", When I have learnt what pro - gress has been
made in mo - dern gun - ne - ry, When I know more of tac - tics than a
accel.
nov - ice in a nun - ne - ry— In short, when I've a smat - ter - ing of
Vivace
el - e - men - tal stra - te - gy—
You'll say a bet - ter Ma - jor - Gen - er -

f Chorus
-al has nev - er sat a gee— You'll say a bet - ter Ma - jor - Gen - er -
-al has nev - er sat a gee, You'll say a bet - ter Ma - jor - Gen - er -
-al has nev - er sat a gee, You'll say a bet - ter Ma - jor - Gen - er -
-al has nev - er sat a, sat a gee.
fz

4. For my mi - li - ta - ry know - ledge, tho' I'm
pp
pluck - y and ad - ven - tu - ry, Has on - ly been brought down to the be -
- gin - ning of the cen - tu - ry; But still, in mat - ters ve - ge - ta - ble,
an - i - mal, and mi - ne - ral, I am the ve - ry mo - del of a

Chorus
f
mo - dern Ma - jor - Gen - er - al. But still, in mat - ters ve - ge - ta - ble,
an - i - mal, and mi - ne - ral, He is the ve - ry mo - del of a
mo - dern Ma - jor - Gen - er - al.
ff

The Nightmare Song
(When You're Lying Awake With A Dismal Headache)

Words by W.S. Gilbert
Music by Sir Arthur Sullivan

lan - guage you choose to in - dulge in, with - out im - pro - pri - e - ty; For your
brain is on fire the bed - clothes con - spire of us - u - al slum - ber to
plun - der you: First your coun - ter - pane goes, and un - cov - ers your toes, and your
sheet slips de - mure - ly from un - der you; Then the blan - ket - ing tick - les— you

feel like mixed pick - les— so ter - ri - bly sharp is the prick - ing, And you're
hot, and you're cross, and you tum - ble and toss till there's no - thing 'twixt you and the
tick - ing. Then the bed - clothes all creep to the ground in a heap, and you
pick 'em all up in a tan - gle; Next your pil - low re - signs and po -

-lite - ly de - clines to re - main at its us - u - al an - gle! Well, you
get some re - pose in the form of a doze, with hot eye - balls and head ev - er
ach - ing, But your slum - ber - ing teems with such hor - ri - ble dreams that you'd
ve - ry much bet - ter be wak - ing; For you dream you are cross - ing the
pp

Chan - nel, and toss - ing a - bout in a steam - er from Har - wich— Which is
some - thing be - tween a large bath - ing ma - chine and a ve - ry small se - cond - class
car - riage— And you're giv - ing a treat (pen - ny ice and cold meat) to a
par - ty of friends and re - la - tions— They're a rav - en - ous horde— and they

all came on board at Sloane Square and South Ken - sing - ton Sta - tions. And
bound on that jour - ney you find your at - tor - ney (who start - ed that morn - ing from
Dev - on); He's a bit un - der - siz'd, and you don't feel sur - pris'd when he
fz
tells you he's on - ly e - lev - en. Well, you're driv - ing like mad with this

sin - gu - lar lad (by - the - bye, the ship's now a four - wheel - er), And you're
play - ing round games, and he calls you bad names when you tell him that "ties pay the
deal - er"; But this you can't stand, so you throw up your hand, and you
find you're as cold as an i - ci - cle; In your shirt and your socks (the black

silk with gold clocks), cross - ing Sal's - bu - ry Plain on a bi - cy - cle: And
he and the crew are on bi - cy - cles too— which they've some - how or oth - er in -
- vest - ed in— And he's tell - ing the tars all the par - tic - u - lars of a
com - pa - ny he's in - ter - est - ed in— It's a scheme of de - vi - ces, to
p

get at low pri - ces all goods from cough mix - tures to ca - bles (Which
tick - led the sai - lors), by treat - ing re - tail - ers as though they were all ve - ge -
- ta - bles– You get a good spades - man to plant a small trades - man (first
take off his boots with a boot - tree), And his legs will take root, and his

fin - gers will shoot, and they'll blos - som and bud like a fruit - tree— From the
green - gro - cer tree you get grapes and green - pea, cau - li - flow - er, pine - ap - ple, and
cran - ber - ries, while the pas - try - cook plant cher - ry bran - dy will grant, ap - ple
puffs, and three - cor - ners, and Ban - bu - rys— The shares are a pen - ny, and
sempre p

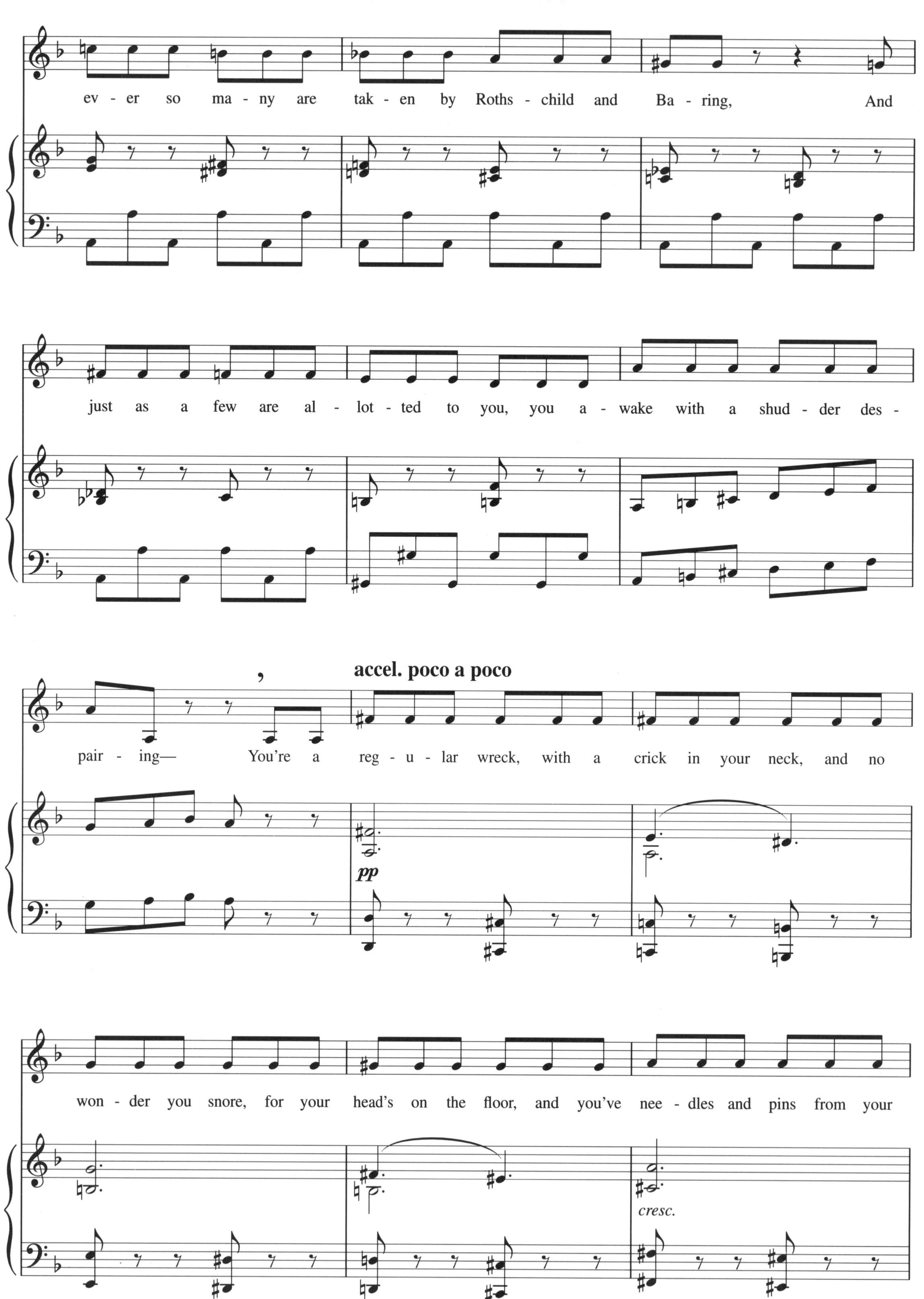
ev - er so ma - ny are tak - en by Roths - child and Ba - ring, And
just as a few are al - lot - ted to you, you a - wake with a shud - der des -
accel. poco a poco
pair - ing— You're a reg - u - lar wreck, with a crick in your neck, and no
pp
won - der you snore, for your head's on the floor, and you've nee - dles and pins from your
cresc.

soles to your shins, and your flesh is a - creep, for your left leg's a - sleep, and you've
cramp in your toes, and a fly on your nose, and some fluff in your lung, and a
dim.
fe - ver - ish tongue, and a thirst that's in - tense, and a gen - er - al sense that you
have - n't been sleep - ing in clo - ver;
But the
cresc.

♩. = 120
dark - ness has pass'd, and it's day - light at last, and the
night has been long— dit - to, dit - to my song—
cresc.
a piacere
Con fuoco
And thank good - ness they're both of them o - ver!
f colla voce
ff

On A Tree By A River
(Willow, Tit Willow)

Words by W.S. Gilbert
Music by Sir Arthur Sullivan

'Wil - low, tit - wil - low, tit - wil - low'?_ Is it weak - ness of in - tel - lect,
bird - ie?" I cried, "Or a ra - ther tough worm in your lit - tle in - side?" With a
shake of his poor lit - tle head he re - plied, "Oh, wil - low, tit - wil - low, tit -
- wil - low!"_ 2. He

slapped at his chest, as he sat on that bough, sing - ing, "Wil - low, tit - wil - low, tit -
p
- wil - low!"_ And a cold per - spi - ra - tion be - span - gled his brow, oh,
wil - low, tit - wil - low, tit - wil - low!_ He__ sobbed and he sighed, and a
gur - gle he gave, then he plunged him - self in - to the

bil - lo - wy wave, and an ec - ho a - rose from the su - i - cide's grave— "Oh,
wil - low, tit - wil - low, tit - wil - low!"
3. Now I feel just as sure as I'm sure that my name is - n't
wil - low, tit - wil - low, tit - wil - low, That 'twas

blight - ed af - fec - tion that made him ex - claim, "Oh, wil - low, tit - wil - low, tit -
- wil - low!"_ And if you re - main cal - lous and ob - du - rate, I shall_
rall.
per - ish as he did, and you will know why, though I pro - ba - bly shall not ex -
claim as I die, "Oh, wil - low, tit - wil - low, tit - wil - low!"_
pp
Ped.

Take A Pair Of Sparkling Eyes

Words by W.S. Gilbert
Music by Sir Arthur Sullivan

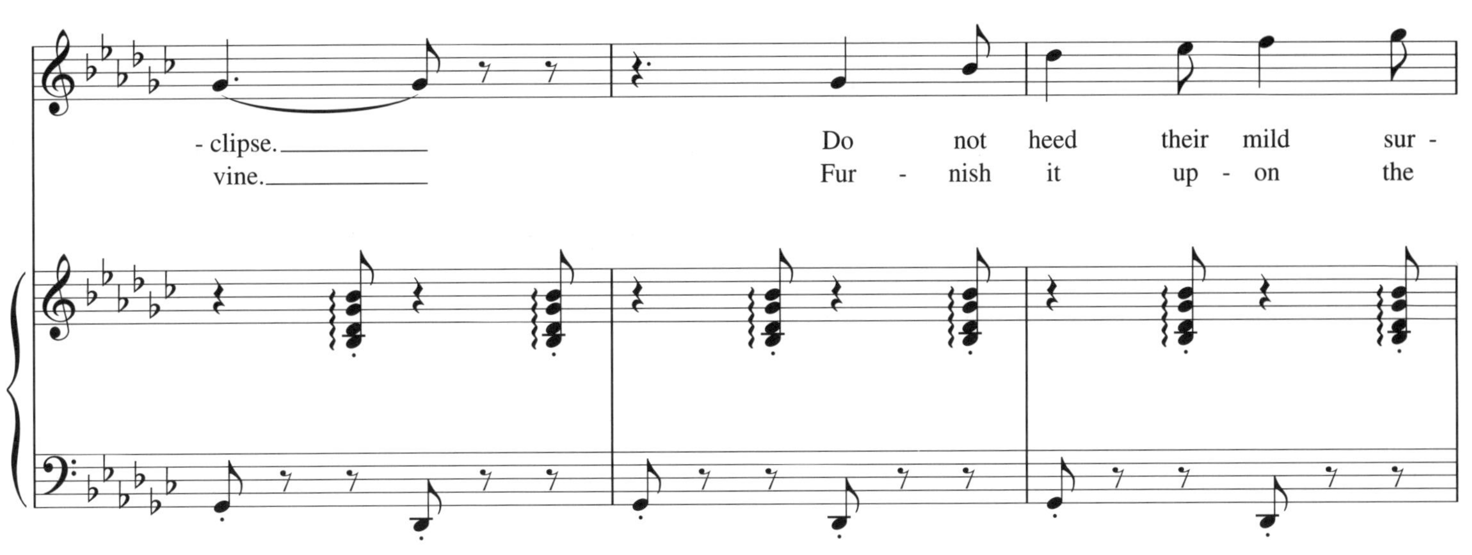
-clipse. Do not heed their mild sur-
vine. Fur-nish it up-on the

-prise, Hav-ing passed the Ru-bi-con. Take a
spot, With the treas-ures rich and rare I've en-

pair of ro-sy lips. Take a fig-ure trim-ly
-deav-oured to de-fine. Live to love and love to

planned,_ Such as ad - mi - ra - tion whets___ (Be par -
live,___ You will ri - pen at your ease,___ Grow - ing
-tic - u - lar in this); Take a ten - der lit - tle
on the sun - ny side, Fate has noth - ing more to
hand,___ Fringed with dain - ty fin - ger - ettes,_ Press___
give.___ You're a dain - ty man to please_ If___

it, press it, in pa-ren-the-sis, Ah!
you're not sat-is-fied, not sat-is-fied. Ah!
sf
Take all
Take my
p
f
dim.
p
these, you luc-ky man, Take and keep them if you
coun-sel, hap-py man; Act up-on it, if you
dim.
p

can, if you can! Take all these, you luc - ky
can, if you can! take my coun - sel, hap - py
man, Take and keep them if you
man; Act up - on it, if you
can, if you can!
can, if you can!
1.
2.
f
Take my coun - sel, hap - py man!

Act up - on it, if you
can, if you can, if you can, Act up - on it, if you
cresc.
Con forza
can, hap - py man, if you can!
Ped.

When All Night Long A Chap Remains

Words by W.S. Gilbert
Music by Sir Arthur Sullivan

-no - to - ny He ex - er - cis - es of his brains, that
-bel - lum, too, They've got to leave that brain out - side, and
accel. poco a poco
is, as - sum - ing that he's got an - y. Tho' nev - er nur - tured
vote just as their lead - ers tell 'em to. But then the pros - pect
in the lap of lux - u - ry, yet I ad - mon - ish you, I
of a lot of dull M. P.'s in close prox - im - i - ty, all
am an in - tel - lec - tual chap, and think of things that would as -
think - ing for them - selves, is what no man can face with e - qua -

rall.
Tempo I° ♩ = 69
-ton - ish you. I of - ten think it's com - i - cal—
-nim - i - ty. Then let's re - joice with loud Fal, lal—
p
Fal, lal, la! Fal, lal, la! How na - ture al - ways
Fal, lal, la! Fal, lal, la! That
does con - trive— Fal, lal, la, la! That ev - 'ry boy and
ev - 'ry gal that's born in - to the world a - live Is

poco rit.
ei - ther a lit - tle Lib - er - al or else a lit - tle Con - ser - va - tive!
a tempo
rit.
Fal, lal, la! Fal, lal, la! Is ei - ther a lit - tle Lib - er - al or
mf
3
a tempo
else a lit - tle Con - ser - va - tive! Fal, lal, la!
colla voce
ff
1.
2.
2. When

I'm Called Little Buttercup

Words by W.S. Gilbert
Music by Sir Arthur Sullivan

still I'm called But - ter - cup, poor Lit - tle But - ter - cup, sweet Lit - tle But - ter - cup
I! I've snuff and to - bac - cy, and ex - cel - lent jac - ky, I've
scis - sors, and watch - es and knives; I've rib - bons and la - ces to
set off the fa - ces of pret - ty young sweet - hearts and wives. I've

trea - cle and tof - fee, I've tea and I've cof - fee, soft
tom - my and suc - cu - lent chops; I've chick - ens and
rall.
co - nies, and pret - ty po - lo - nies, and ex - cel - lent pep - per - mint
a tempo
drops. Then buy of your But - ter - cup, dear Lit - tle

But - ter - cup, Sai - lors should nev - er be shy; So
buy of your But - ter - cup, poor Lit - tle But - ter - cup, come, of your
But - ter - cup buy.
colla voce
f

Poor Wand'ring One!

Words by W.S. Gilbert
Music by Sir Arthur Sullivan

a tempo
one!
Poor wan - d'ring one!
If such poor love as mine
rall.
Can help thee find true peace of mind—
Why, take it, it is thine!
Chorus
Take heart,

no dan - ger low'rs; Take an - y heart— but
ours! Take heart, fair days will shine; Take
an - y heart— take mine!
Chorus
Take
heart, no dan - ger low'rs; Take an - y

heart— but ours! Take heart, fair days will
shine; take an - y heart— take mine! Ah!
Ah! Ah!
p
cresc.
Ah!
f

a tempo
Poor wan - d'ring one!
Tho' thou hast
p
sure - ly stray'd,
Take heart of
rall.
grace, thy steps re - trace,
Poor wan - d'ring
a tempo
one!
Ah, ah!
Ah, ah,
p

ah!
Ah, ah!
Ah, ah, ah!
Fair days will shine,
Take
heart!
8va
pp
(8)

8va
Take
mine!
Take
heart!
p
pp
8va
(8)

a tempo
Take mine!
f
Ah! Ah!
tr
cadenza ad lib.
Ah!
Take heart!
ff
Ped.

The Sun Whose Rays Are All Ablaze

Words by W.S. Gilbert
Music by Sir Arthur Sullivan

But, fierce and bold, In fie - ry gold, He glo - ries all ef - ful - gent.
I
mean to rule the earth, as he the sky—
We real - ly know our worth,
The sun and I!
cresc.
I mean to rule the earth, as he the sky— We
dim.
rall.
a tempo
real - ly know our worth, the sun and I!
mf
p sostenuto

Ob - serve his flame, that pla - cid dame, the moon's Ce - les - tial High - ness;
There's not a trace up - on her face of dif - fi - dence or shy - ness:
She bor - rows light that, thro' the night, Man - kind may all ac - claim her!
And, truth to tell, She lights up well; So I, for one, don't blame her.

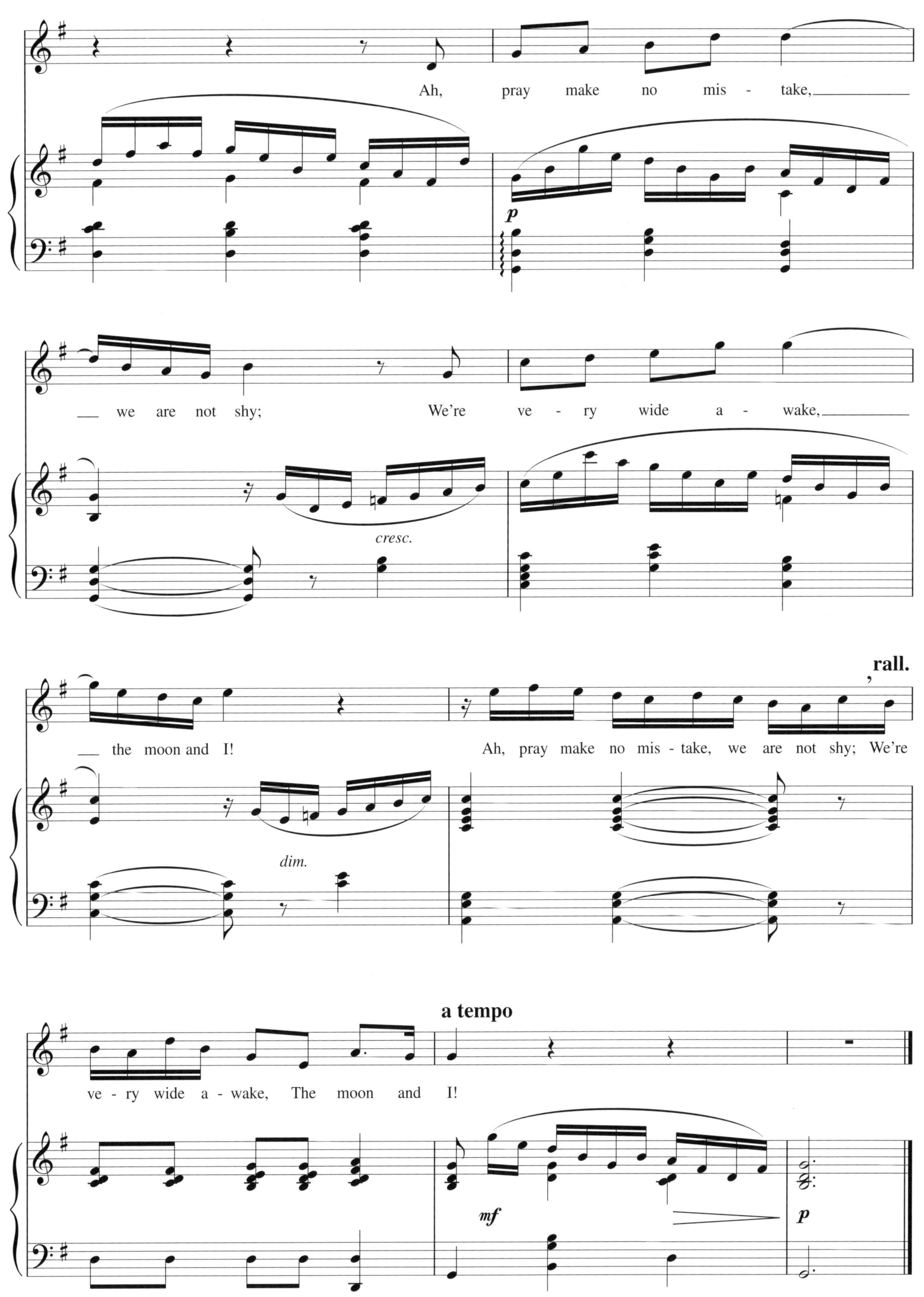
Ah, pray make no mis - take,
we are not shy;
We're ve - ry wide a - wake,
the moon and I!
Ah, pray make no mis - take, we are not shy; We're
ve - ry wide a - wake, The moon and I!
p
cresc.
rall.
dim.
a tempo
mf
p

When Maiden Loves She Sits And Sighs

Words by W.S. Gilbert
Music by Sir Arthur Sullivan

wan - ders to and fro; Un - bid - den tear - drops fill her eyes, and
owl mopes on a tree; Al - though she keen - ly feels the smart, she
to all ques - tions she re - plies, with a sad "Heigh ho!"
can - not tell what ails her heart, with its sad "Ah, me!"
meno mosso
'Tis but a lit - tle word— "Heigh ho!"
'Tis but a fool - ish sigh— "Ah, me!"

a tempo
So soft, 'tis scarce - ly heard— "Heigh ho!" An i - dle breath— Yet
Born but to droop and die— "Ah, me!" Yet all the sense Of
life and— death may hang up - on a maid's "Heigh ho!"
el - o - quence lies hid - den in a maid's "Ah, me!"
rit.
An i - dle breath— Yet life and death may hang up - on a maid's— "Heigh
Yet all the sense— Of el - o - quence lies hid - den in a maid's— "Ah,

1. a tempo
- ho!"
2.
me!" "Ah, me!" "Ah, me!"
Yet all the sense of el - o - quence lies hid - den in a maid's "Ah,
colla voce
a tempo
me!"

Silvered Is The Raven Hair

Words by W.S. Gilbert
Music by Sir Arthur Sullivan

rall.
bye! Lit - tle will be left of me, In the com - ing bye and
a tempo
bye!
Fad - ing is the ta - per waist, shape - less grows the
shape - ly limb, and al - though se - vere - ly laced, spread - ing is the

fig - ure trim! Stout - er than I used to be, still more cor - pu -
rall.
a tempo
- lent grow I— There will be too much of me in the com - ing by and
p
bye!
f
There will be too much of me in the com - ing by, and
appassionato
ff
mf
a tempo
bye!
f